101 Girl Tips

Lisa Tiano
and
Carly Hartman

Copyright ©2017 by Lisa Tiano and Carly Hartman

All rights reserved. No portion of this book may be reproduced – mechanically, electronically, or by any other means, including photocopying – without written permission of the publisher.

Printed in the United States of America
First Printing, 2017
ISBN-10: 1545326398
ISBN-13: 978-1545326398

This book is dedicated to all the girls and young women who are our future leaders of the 21st century. This is YOUR time to make positive changes in your life, and to live happily and peacefully. Rise above the challenges you face and go for it!

ACKNOWLEDGMENTS

Thank You are the two golden words that express how grateful we are. As part of our journey in writing this book, we appreciate our family and friends who have supported us every step of the way. Thank you so much for believing in us.

We want to thank all the girls who have shared with us over the years. Whether during workshops, conferences, school assemblies, private groups, or pageants, please know that we have learned as much from you as you have learned from us. We appreciate your honesty and open communication. Your input and stories you've shared remind us how important every girl's individual journey is, as well as the obstacles and challenges that girl's face on a daily basis.

With love and gratitude,

Lisa and Carly

101 Girl Tips was created to be an inspirational guide for all girls and young women. Coping, learning new ways of living fearlessly and with confidence is our hope for all girls.

A HUGE thank you to Wendy Hernandez, who edited this book from beginning to end! What a special person and friend to have done this for us!

A very special thank you to my daughters, Brynn Tiano and Mia Tiano for showing your love, laughs, and support every single day. My inspiration in writing this book had much to do with the both of you. Your humbleness and ability to show that kindness is the coolest quality to have is incredible! You've taught me the biggest lesson in life, and something that any mother would be grateful to learn – how to love unconditionally. I'm so proud of the young women you've become, and knowing the importance of always staying true to who you are. To my husband, Al Tiano, thank you for believing in me and your endless support all these years as I continue to take more risks and follow my dreams. If I had to choose one amazing thing about you, it would be your sense of humor and compassion that gives us all a better sense of life. I'm so grateful for our marriage and love which have allowed me to go confidently in the direction of my dreams!

And lastly, I would be remiss in not thanking my dad, who is unfortunately no longer here on this earth, but forever in my heart. It was my dad who told me for many years that he believed in me and that I should be writing books to help and inspire others. So, here I am, three years since his passing, and fulfilling that promise with all my heart.

♥ Lisa

Contents

Beauty & Body Image 1

Confidence 27

Fear 49

Friendship 67

Lifestyle 87

My Journey Follows 115

About the Authors:

Insightful, compassionate and inspiring, Lisa Tiano thrives on educating and building her connection with the pre-teen and teenage population. For over two decades, Lisa has used her knowledge and education, having a Master's degree in Clinical Psychology, and guiding a community of girls with essential life skills to become confident leaders and role models. With her forward thinking, cutting edge knowledge, and her ability to empower girls and young women to reach their highest potential, Lisa provides strategic, hands-on tools in her workshops and assemblies that enable girls to succeed in every aspect of their lives. Her copyrighted curriculum has been fundamental for special programming in schools and organizations that focus on the social changes of our generation of girls. Lisa is a parenting consultant, speaker, leadership trainer and founder of *InnerStarGirl and REAL Teen Talk*. She is the mother of two teen daughters, ages 13 and 16, and married for 20 years. Please visit Lisa at her websites and blog:

www.innerstargirl.com and www.mompersonal.com

As CEO and creator of Pageant 360, Carly Hartman has always had a passion and a desire in her heart to change the world. She believes one of the first ways to head in this direction is to help young women. There are so many women who do not believe in themselves. They go through life thinking that they are not worthy of anything. It is Carly's vision to change this across the world. She wants young women to know, from the bottom of their hearts, that they are beautiful, valuable, and have a purpose. Carly will accomplish this goal and fight for women in this way, no matter what it takes.

Please visit Carly at www.pageant360.com

Beauty & Body Image

The Wisdom of Loving Yourself

No. 1

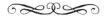

The first step to accepting and respecting your body is recognizing what you like about your body shape and knowing that perfection is not a realistic standard by which to live. There is no such thing as a perfect body, no matter what the media portrays on television and in magazines. Images in the media are altered, enhanced and airbrushed, and far from realistic.

No. 2

Did you know that more than 80% of 10-year-old girls are afraid of being considered fat? By the time they get to middle school, more than 50% of girls are dissatisfied with at least two of their own body parts. Give yourself realistic goals to achieve, and start using positive language. Without using words like "I'm so fat" or "I hate my thighs," change the way you talk about yourself. Be kind to yourself.

No. 3

Too many girls want to be "model thin," which is no surprise when girls are exposed to countless images of stick figure models and celebrities. Keep in mind, these are not real-life role models. The supermodel figure is not the norm. Know that the average female is not a size two or four. The supermodel might be pretty on the outside, but you don't know the real person behind the runway, nor do you know what she's going through.

No. 4

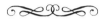

Embrace the fact that your body is changing. Hello, pimples and acne! Let's face it, many pre-teens and teens go through that awkward phase of the occasional breakout. So, don't allow others to make fun of your uncompromising complexion. You're not alone. Many girls experience acne or skin conditions. The good news is, there are many over-the-counter products that can help. Or, you might want to consult with an aesthetician, skin specialist, or your physician to help you.

No. 5

More than 40% of girls in high school attempt to lose weight because they're not satisfied with how they look. Keeping healthy is the most important thing you can do for yourself. It's not about the scale, or what you weigh. It's about feeling good and keeping a healthy weight that's appropriate for your height and body type.

No. 6

Participating in a sport or activity you love is so important! Staying healthy and fit is great for your mind and body and helps keep a positive attitude. Any activity you enjoy helps with the way you feel about yourself. So, find an activity you like and look forward to playing, and not something that you dread doing!

No. 7

It's not healthy to envy another girl's appearance. While it's okay to appreciate how fit or stylish someone is, you don't need to be hard on yourself. It's more important to feel secure in who you are, embrace what you look like, and not always want to try and look like someone else. Wouldn't it be a little boring if we all looked the same? You weren't born to blend in. You were born to stand out!

No. 8

Age is precious. You are your current age for a reason. Don't feel pressured by society to look older than your actual age. So many girls and young women try too hard to look older than they actually are. You are only your current age for one year, so appreciate it and enjoy every minute of it! There is no need to look like you're 30 when you're only 14. Old age will come, so appreciate your youth now!

No. 9

Girls are notorious for finding fault with themselves. "I wish I was taller, thinner, smarter." It's like wanting to break free from self-critical prison. Try this one strategy and do your best to practice it: Think about the qualities you like about yourself. Write them down in a little notebook or journal. Before you go to bed at night, read your own positive notes. Try adding to your journal weekly.

No. 10

A lot of girls are guilty of hiding behind their hair. Even the most beautiful hair is not meant to act as a shield or security blanket. Try wearing your hair up some days, or try different styles. Encourage yourself to experiment with your hair, and try out different styles without hiding from the outside world!

No. 11

Your beauty is not defined by the number of people who like you. You are beautiful no matter what others think of you. Beauty goes skin deep. What makes you beautiful is the person you are, which is built on character and values . Someone can be beautiful in appearance, but be the most miserable and unkind person. A good personality is the most attractive trait any girl can have!

No. 12

It's tempting to compare yourself to others. The problem with this is, not everyone grows and develops the same, nor at the same pace - especially in going through puberty. Puberty can cause many changes in the body. Everyone also has different body types. Short, tall, thin, curvy. So, it's not fair to compare yourself to other people.

No. 13

Trying to achieve a summer body can sometimes feel stressful, especially if you're giving yourself a short amount of time to work at it. Why not work on your summer body all year long so that there isn't so much pressure you put on yourself? Pace yourself throughout the year. Try to be mindful, make healthy choices, and do some sort of physical activity on a regular basis so that you don't overdo it or injure yourself. You'll be able to achieve your summer body in due time, while also feeling good that you're doing something positive for yourself.

No. 14

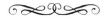

Are you someone who's always being so self-critical? Stop saying the word "if." If I didn't have these freckles. If I didn't have a round face. If I didn't have these big feet. Find what features you *do* like about yourself. Is it your big, beautiful eyes, full lips, or shapely calves? Try not to fixate on the things you don't like about yourself and appreciate what you *do* like.

No. 15

Are you looking for constant feedback on social media? How many selfies do you think you take in a 24-hour period? And how many do you take before you post that "perfect" picture? Are your followers commenting on your posts? Don't look for validation from others. You'll always be waiting for that perfect response. And what if you don't receive it? The point is, don't sit around waiting for others to validate who you are. You already know who you are. Embrace who you are without depending on feedback from others.

No. 16

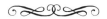

Whether you think you're beautiful or not, you need to focus on your heart. Are you a person who likes to give to others? Are you generous, thoughtful, and sensitive? It's time to love yourself and appreciate the qualities that make you unique. Think about the attributes and character traits that make you the special person you are.

No. 17

Truly, there's no need to hide behind your makeup. So many girls and women cake it on, hence appearing like "cakeface." It's okay to enhance your natural beauty with a little makeup, but no need to overdo it. Besides, the less you wear, the less time it takes to get ready for school, and that's a good thing. High school can be the perfect time to start exploring with cosmetics. On the other hand, you may discover that you feel more comfortable without wearing any makeup at all!

No. 18

It's important to surround yourself with positive friends, and friends who support you and lift you up, rather than friends who bring you down or who are full of insults. If you have a friend who constantly judges the way you look, or criticizes the clothes you wear, it might be time to give that friend a break. The friends who you choose can either be a healthy influence or a bad influence. Find your tribe and choose your friends wisely.

No. 19

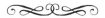

Whenever you start feeling down about yourself, thinking you're not good enough, pretty enough, or smart enough, realize that many girls your same age feel exactly the way you do. So, don't throw yourself a pity party! The way you snap out of it is to go out of your comfort zone. You probably have friends who feel the same way, and perhaps they're self-critical as well. Try giving someone you know a compliment, or give a friend a hug. Maybe even point out their beautiful features. You'll realize how quickly *you'll* feel better about yourself, while making that other person feel good too!

No. 20

The most important thing to remember when it comes to makeup is wearing what's best for your skin type, and not what all your other friends are using. You may find yourself buying the wrong makeup for your skin type. While you think it may be flattering, overusing or purchasing the wrong products can actually do more damage to your skin. Breakouts, blemishes and other skin flare ups can be caused by a variety of reasons. Go easy on the makeup, or consult with a dermatologist, and first find out if you have normal, oily, or dry skin before you spend all that money on cosmetics!

No. 21

Just like a painting, treat your skin like a fresh canvas. The best skin care tip any girl can receive is to find a good skin care regimen. Instead of being self-critical about your complexion, know that hormonal changes can affect your face and body. A simple rule of thumb, and one of the best kept secrets in taking care of your skin is to find a good facial cleanser and use it daily.

No. 22

Social media exaggerates. Photos you see on social media sites are usually filtered, cropped, edited or airbrushed. That means that what you actually see is oftentimes not real. There is no need for comparison between you and someone else in a photo. Live life free of insecurities and harsh judgment against yourself.

No. 23

There are all different kinds of builds and body types. Everyone is built differently, so comparing your body to someone else is neither fair to yourself nor worth it. Keep in mind that you don't know another person's lifestyle that you're comparing yourself to. That girl you're idolizing who you think has the perfect body may have a very unhealthy way of living life. Remember, you're not walking in that other person's shoes.

Confidence

Essential Tips for Knowing and Trusting Yourself

No. 24

When you walk into a room with confidence, you will automatically command the attention of others. People will naturally gravitate towards you because they sense the confidence you carry. Believe it or not, your body language speaks volumes—your eye contact, your arms, how you stand and walk say a lot about you.

No. 25

Don't be afraid to give your opinion on a topic. Know that what you say adds value to a conversation and projects confidence. What you think and say portrays you as a leader rather than a follower who just goes along with the popular vote. Show that your opinion matters. Know that your opinion matters, not just to a crowd, but to yourself.

No. 26

Being confident means walking the walk, not just talking the talk. Your mom wasn't trying to be annoying when she kept yelling, "No slouching and sit up straight!" She was right. People can sense your mood even with your posture. It's knowing that when you walk into a room, people will notice how inviting you are, and walking with confidence is a great trait! So, your mother's words hold value. Keep your head up high, your shoulders down, and no slouching!

No. 27

Don't be afraid to flex your voice muscles. It's better to be a stand-up person than a bystander who just listens and watches others from the side lines and does nothing. Making the right choices is all about standing up for what is right. Speak up and state your opinion without feeling you have to sit quietly.

No. 28

Having a vision of your dreams and goals is an excellent way to improve confidence. Try keeping a journal and writing down your goals and things you want to accomplish. Visualization is also one of the most powerful tools for keeping positive. You know that test you've been studying for and want to do well on? Picturing yourself doing well on an exam or envisioning yourself scoring that winning goal are ways of preparing your mind for successful outcomes. Keep visualizing, keep writing down your goals and dreams, and you'll start feeling more self-assured!

No. 29

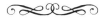

Bye bye, peer pressure! Be who you are and not who someone else wants you to be. Kids often want to fit in and feel accepted. This is why peer pressure is the worst. The last thing you want to do is something that a friend pushes you into doing, then having regrets later. Stay true to who you are and never give in to something you don't feel right about doing.

No. 30

Girls often use someone else's weakness as their weapon. If you're a target of bullying, use your voice muscles and speak up for yourself. Tell the person who's mistreating you that you don't like what they're saying or doing. The sooner you show that you won't put up with meanness, the quicker you'll be known as a person who won't allow others to mistreat you. Respect yourself and your dignity.

No. 31

Know who you are. Confidence is key in making and keeping any healthy friendship or relationship. If you don't like yourself, then how can you expect anyone else to like you? Going through the tween and teen years are one of the most challenging times. Even though girls tend to be self-critical, no girl should be held back in reaching her full potential. Try embracing your unique qualities rather than picking them apart. How you see yourself is how others see you. Look in the mirror and find that beautiful girl inside you.

No. 32

Giving presentations in front of an entire classroom can be terrifying! However, we all have to perform in front of an audience at some point! Why not enjoy the moment while you're presenting? Try being clever, or add in a few funny remarks. Allow yourself to feel relaxed in front of your peers, and prepare for your presentation so you can be natural while just being yourself. Good public speaking takes practice. Your bedroom mirror can be your best friend and audience when practicing!

No. 33

If you have a crush, but you start to realize that he doesn't respect you for who you are, then that is no crush to have! Don't let his good looks and charm fool you. You deserve to be treated with respect, so do not waste your time with someone who doesn't treat you with dignity.

No. 34

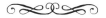

We all get cravings for different types of food. For one person, it might be chocolate or candy. For others, it may be the carb cravings (like pizza or bread). Whatever the weakness is you're wanting to cave into, don't feel like you've just lost a never-ending battle, or not worthy of it. Life is not meant to live with deprivation, or go without enjoying the things we like. Binging or depriving ourselves is the last thing we want to do. So, go ahead and have that slice of pizza or Godiva chocolate and allow yourself what you're craving!

No. 35

Hope. Be confident in the concept of hope and faith. Life is too short to be scared. Sure, we may have fears that we haven't conquered, but that doesn't mean we lose faith or give up. Giving up is not an option. Take the support that others give you. Reach out to family and friends when you *really* need someone. Trust that everything will work out even though you may have doubts now.

No. 36

You are not a definition of your past. No matter what mistakes you may have made, keep moving forward. Don't linger on with what's happened. The past belongs in the past. The future is your second chance, and it is a precious one.

No. 37

When someone calls you "*bossy*", you first need to ask yourself, "am I being self-confident and assertive, or am I talking down to others?" Talking down to people like they're your working staff is not a good trait, and you're more apt to lose friends rather than gain some. Being a leader is admirable and something to be proud of. It's important to be aware and conscientious of how you speak to others around you.

No. 38

It's important to not feel the need to give into peer pressure. You do not have to be like everyone else. You were created to be different. You don't have to go to every party or event, do everything your friends are doing, or go everywhere your friends are going. You can be confident in declining to go along with the crowd. If your friends are not supportive of you, then perhaps they weren't your friends in the first place. If they're your true friends, they will understand how you feel.

No. 39

Sometimes people have confidence issues with asking questions in classroom settings. When you are in that situation, know that you are not alone. Your question is not silly or stupid. Did you know that you might have the *same* question as another one of your classmates? Build up the courage to ask your teacher whatever is you're questioning. This is *your* learning experience, so make it your own!

No. 40

A smile is a wonderful attribute. Even if you're not in the best mood, smiling can improve the way you feel. The pure act of smiling and using those muscles has the capacity to produce happy chemicals in the brain. Your smile also has the ability to attract others around you. Try smiling more. Notice the positive reactions you'll receive.

No. 41

No matter what might be happening around you, never forget to view it with a positive attitude. Positivity can oftentimes make all the difference because of how you approach a problem. Try not to let fear have a hold on you or keep you down. Having a positive attitude may be hard during a difficult time, but being optimistic shows you're able to face the problem head on. Use the same positive manner with yourself like you do with a friend. I'm sure when you try to help someone that you're positive in your approach. Be optimistic with yourself too!

No. 42

Try not to say "*I get it*" when speaking to someone. What that tends to mean is "*you don't have to speak anymore.*" Allow the person to finish talking, and don't ever assume you know how they are going to finish their sentences. Confidence and respect go hand in hand. Confidently allow others to share what it is they're trying to communicate. Be a good listener and be patient, just as you would like them to do when you speak.

No. 43

Having good self-esteem and feeling confident makes it a lot easier in making new friends. When you're self-assured and feel good about yourself, it makes you more approachable to others. Your thoughts might be holding you back. "No one will talk to me," or, "They'll think I'm weird." You are your own worst enemy by thinking negatively. So, try challenging those bad thoughts and paying attention to your outward appearance, making sure you come across as welcoming.

Fear

Transforming Fear Into Action

No. 44

Public speaking or speaking up in general is a huge fear for many girls. Take for example, a school presentation or oral report. This can cause classroom jitters for any student! It's not that you're unprepared. It's the fear of speaking in front of peers and teachers and feeling anxious that you might mess up in the middle of a class speech. Or, it could be the fear of being judged. Don't think you're the only one feeling this anxiety. Many kids feel the same way, and these situations can be stressful for anyone. Perhaps you can share your feelings with friends who are in the same boat as you. Help each other and cheer each other on for your next speech!

No. 45

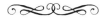

Fear of change is very common. Everyone naturally feels more comfortable with a routine. After all, routines are consistent and something that you've been doing for quite some time. Change isn't always easy. Whether it's having to change schools, or a move to another house, or changing from one sport to another to try something different, that's exactly what it is— different. Different is often good, but understandably, we get into a comfort zone and change feels kind of weird. The adjustment will come with time. Take one day at a time.

No. 46

We all know that it's impossible to please everyone, all the time—family, friends, teachers, or anyone who is in your life that you care about. So, the fear of letting down those we are closest to is a valid feeling. Fear of disappointing parents is huge in girl world. Your parents love you and do so much for you every single day. No one is perfect. Not you, not your parents, friends or anyone else for that matter. So, don't think you can satisfy everyone in your life 100% of the time. Accept that you won't be able to fulfill everyone's needs.

No. 47

Find the courage within you to speak up. Sometimes in situations, people around you might say things you don't agree with. Guess what? You have just as much right to speak up as they do! Your feelings are important, so don't be afraid to use your voice. If you don't say something when you feel the need to, you might regret it later.

No. 48

Trying out for a school sport? It can be quite stressful, especially if you haven't been playing that sport for a long time. Think of it this way—there are so many girls just like you who are trying out for a sport. They feel the same way as you do. How courageous of you that you took this huge leap and are making the effort of being part of a team sport! It's normal to be fearful and anxious, thinking the worst, "What if I don't make it?" But what if you *do*? Put your best foot forward, and maybe take lessons if you can before you try out for any team so you're well prepared.

No. 49

Relationships between boys and girls are very confusing. Many teenage girls fear never being able to find love. Like a fairytale or romance novel, girls yearn to find their true love companion. On the other hand, many girls are scared of entering into any sort of relationship. Fear of being rejected is common, just as much as fear of commitment. Feelings of attraction, passion, and romance are full of excitement, but it can also be confusing and scary. Slow down, stop and think. There's no race, nor is there a romance marathon!

No. 50

Being bullied is a big issue. Whether it's being cyber bullied, or being bullied emotionally, socially or physically, it can take a toll on any person. This can happen at any age, but it's important to share these situations if they're occurring at school or outside of school. The hidden aggression will only get worse if you don't talk about it with your parent or school staff. They will help you get through it, and the important thing is to not be afraid of reporting the issue. Not speaking up or reporting the incidences will only make matters worse. Take that first step and talk about it with a trusted adult.

No. 51

Anxiety about school and grades is a common worry. The truth is, comparing yourself to how other friends do academically is the worst thing you can do. It's also unrealistic—simply because everyone learns differently, and at a different pace. Homework, tests, grades and fear of failing or doing poorly are all normal school stressors, but it's important to catch things early. So, if you feel you need help in a certain subject, talk to your parent or school counselor immediately. Don't feel like you have to struggle alone.

No. 52

For many girls, the pre-teen and teenage years are almost always full of worries and fear. No one has a completely worry-free life. Not even adults! It's common for girls to worry about what others think of them—what friends think of how you look and how you dress. This is because wanting to fit in and be part of a group is a huge desire for many girls. Desire or not, try to think of yourself as different from and more unique than everyone else. True friends will respect you and accept you for who you are, no matter what you look like or interests you have.

No. 53

Knowing how to deal with failure and not give up are definitely positive traits. Sure, it's difficult when you see yourself fail at something. Whether it's a test at school or a game you lost, having a winning attitude can make all the difference. Failing doesn't mean you've failed at life. Building self-confidence takes work and learning from failure is certainly not effortless. No one ever said being successful was easy.

No. 54

This may sound embarrassing, but fear of being left alone at night, or being afraid of the dark are realistic fears. Not just for little kids. Many tween and teen girls, as well as adults, suffer from insomnia, and are not able to fall sleep easily. Poor sleepers might have difficulty having the lights completely turned off, and then their imaginations prevent them from feeling safe. Having nightlights or some cool, soothing room lighting can often help.

No. 55

Fear is usually the root of all decisions in life. Fear can also hold you back from pursuing your dreams and goals. Do you base all your decisions on fear? Try taking little steps and confronting some of your fears – or maybe just one fear. You might surprise yourself at how you're able to conquer things you thought you would never be able to do in the first place.

No. 56

What would you do in life if you didn't have any fear? Start a club? Pursue an activity? Join an organization? The possibilities are endless. Try thinking about something you've been wanting to do for a long time, but have been holding yourself back for whatever reason. What if you took a leap and tried doing one thing you've had your heart set on doing? It might actually be the best thing you've ever done for yourself!

No. 57

When you find yourself afraid of something, really analyze your feelings. Are you just afraid or perhaps just nervous and excited? Being slightly "good" nervous and excited are positive feelings to have. So, if you find yourself in that position, realize that excitement is something to embrace and look forward to.

No. 58

Sometimes certain fears can linger into the teenage and adult years. For example, if you experienced fear of darkness when you were a child, did you ever give thought about how much this is holding you back? Being afraid of the dark could have been a result of something you experienced from the past. Maybe you went on a scary ride at an amusement park when you were younger and it affected you, causing you not to go to on park rides at night. Sometimes, getting over our fears takes time. Be patient, and don't allow that one fear from the past to affect you and keep you from enjoying the rest of your life.

No. 59

Fear of losing friends and being let down is common. Many kids gossip and spread rumors, attacking someone's social status. This could have happened to you, where you feel like no one will talk to you or be your friend because of something that someone else said about you. First, establish what the rumor is, and if what was said is even valid. Consider the source of where it came from. Many times, girls make pointless efforts in worrying about their reputations, when most reputations speak for themselves. If most people know you're a loyal, trustworthy, good friend, then they'll realize the gossipers are just stirring up trouble for no reason.

Friendship

Keeping Company With the Right People

No. 60

Just because your best friend isn't talking to you doesn't mean she's over you. Maybe she's just having a bad day, or there's something else you're not aware of. If the friendship means that much to you, talk to her about it rather than avoid the issue. She might just want some breathing room, but confronting rather than guessing will keep you from losing a good night's sleep.

No. 61

Two friends of yours get into an argument. They try to bring you into it, wanting you to take sides. You like them both equally, but don't want to get in the middle, nor hurt anyone's feelings. *Do not* allow yourself to get caught in a web. Tell them openly and honestly that you care for them both and explain that they can work it out, just the two of them, *if* they hear what each person has to say. If they're really good friends, they'll understand how dragging you into their problem is not the answer.

No. 62

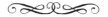

If you found out your friends are having a sleepover and you weren't invited, don't just pretend that you didn't find out. Honesty is the best policy rather than covering up your true feelings. Tell them you're hurt and not sure why you weren't included. There could have been a misunderstanding. Or, you just might discover that these weren't your true girlfriends after all. Better to find out now than later.

No. 63

What girl doesn't have some sort of pressure in her life from either a friend, parent or relative? There are so many added pressures of being a young girl in today's world - the pressures of school and academics, homework load, the social pressures that girls put on themselves of having to "fit in," and friends' expectations. But, what about the pressures you put on yourself? Do you ever think, "Maybe I expect too much of myself"?

No. 64

Your friend makes fun of your new sneakers you just bought. Do you let her make you feel awful? Or, do you speak up and say, "Hey, I really like them." Of course, speak up! Let her know you'd never mock her if she just purchased something she liked. Good friends are honest without making a big to-do about something.

No. 65

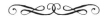

Lately, you notice your good friend is starting to hang out with people you don't care for. You don't want to hurt her feelings and say they're not really your cup of tea. That's the beauty of having different circles of friends - so you don't feel stuck. It's okay that your friend hangs with different people, and it's also okay that you do the same. Spread your wings and find some new friends where you discover you have things in common.

No. 66

A good friend you've known for a long time is now thinking she's just too cool to hang around you at school. Lately, you've been feeling dissed by her. She might not be aware of it, or she could be ignoring you on purpose. The best way to handle this is to talk to her outside of school, without others around. Be honest and tell her how you're feeling, and let her know it's not cool how she's treating you. If she cares enough about your friendship, she'll understand and refrain from treating you like you're invisible.

No. 67

We all know friends can tease and make jokes. Sometimes we hear the all too familiar "just kidding" comments. Even though we hear friends say "just kidding" after commenting, it can often offend and hurt feelings. For example, when a friend says, "your feet are so big, like boats! Just kidding," it can push a sensitive spot if you feel you do have big feet. The last thing you want to do is overreact or get bent out of shape. Honesty is the best policy, so your feelings don't fester for a long time. Tell her how you feel.

No. 68

Your birthday is coming up soon. This year, you decide you don't want to have a huge party and would just prefer to do something small and intimate. What do you do? Well, the last thing you want is to leave people out, and your intention is not to hurt friends. The best thing would be to either do something special with *just* your family, or invite all your friends (without leaving anyone out). Bottom line, "*do unto others as you would have others do unto you.*"

No. 69

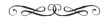

Girls making friends is one of those things in life where it doesn't matter whether you're 12 years old, or 18 or 35. For girls, friends are one of the most important and special things that can change your entire world. Making friends, keeping friends, and building long-lasting friendships are what girls focus on the most. Ask yourself, "what qualities in a friend are important to me?" Hang with friends who make you feel good rather than insecure, and surround yourself with those who bring out the best in you. Remember, the best kinds of friendships are the real ones, where you can just be yourself!

No. 70

It feels so good to have a best friend. In the moments when you just need your bestie to lean on, it really is an incredible feeling to know that a good friend is there for you. It also feels good to give back. So, just as much as you need your friends in good times and bad, it's good to give and be there for them as well.

No. 71

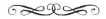

Everyone has friendship challenges. No one friendship is perfect 100% of the time. Friendships often change over time. There's friendship drama, catastrophes, and sometimes social bullying where girls gossip, make fun, exclude, or get other friends to go against one another. This can cause a lot of stress and anxiety, depending on the situation. Getting through middle school and high school can be a tough time, but learning from bad situations and getting out of unhealthy friendships is the best thing you can do for yourself.

No. 72

Many girls want to be in the "in" crowd or feel popular. The best tip is to not push the popularity thing. Find friends who have similar interests and activities that you enjoy. The last thing you want is to get caught up with a crowd of girls who are nothing like you. Choose friends who are supportive and who are a positive influence. You'll be much happier knowing you avoided lots of drama, and that's a very cool thing!

No. 73

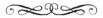

The best way to find yourself in a healthy friendship and not a toxic one is to know the difference between the good ones from the dangerous ones. Good friends look out for each other, have each other's backs, care about one another, include each other in activities and have mutual respect. The bad ones leave you feeling manipulated, hurt or awful about yourself. Prepare yourself for ending those toxic friendships, and don't allow yourself to hang on for what you know is ultimately not a good situation to be in. Never question your self-worth!

No. 74

What does being a good friend mean to you? Are you a good listener? Do you encourage and cheer your friends on? Can you problem solve when you have an argument, so you both don't feel like you're blaming and pointing fingers? Do you respect each other's opinions and differences? Are you fun to be around, or a drag most of the time (hopefully not!)? Think about these questions seriously, and give yourself opportunities to grow and learn, and be that good friend.

No. 75

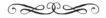

Mean girls and queen bee girls. Ring leaders and girls who stir up most of the drama. Does this sound familiar to you? If you sense you're getting caught up in a group that just doesn't feel right to you, *get out immediately*! Don't wait until you're right in the middle of all the drama. These types of girls have nothing positive to offer you. On the outside, they might appear to be the popular girls. But, really, these girls are nothing more than pot stirrers, and you could never trust them as true friends. Friendship doesn't mean being controlled by bullies. These queen bee girls just want to control and intimidate others.

No. 76

In any good friendship, forgiveness is key. It's normal to get into disagreements, or have misunderstandings with friends. Don't give up so quickly on someone you care about. It's not a game of who apologizes first or who makes the first move in talking. Both of you want to feel better and move on. So, don't be defensive or feel embarrassed, or afraid to initiate conversation with your friend. Talk about your feelings, and listen and hear your friend out too. Nobody's perfect, including you. Friends get hurt, and saying "I'm sorry" says a lot about your character.

Lifestyle

Living Healthy for a Lifetime

No. 77

Social media can be extremely distracting. Most of the time, our eyes are glued to our phone screens. Do not have Fear Of Missing Out (FOMO). You need to separate "fun" time with "work" time. If you have work to get done, the phone needs to be put away or turned off. If you have a few minutes of free time, then use it wisely. Listen to music, read, or just relax. Just know that you can't be on social media all the time. Your eyes, your brain, and *you* deserve a break!

No. 78

It doesn't matter if you're a student in public school or private school. School in general has rigorous academic demands. So, the important question is, how do you prioritize? Most kids have school, extra-curricular activities, homework and other activities. How can you do all of it without running out of energy and time? Often, what helps, is writing down a realistic weekly calendar. Prioritize and differentiate the "Must Do's" from the "Should Do's" and "Want to Do's."

No. 79

The best thing you can do for yourself is to keep your room clean and your space organized. If there is one thing that you need to know about having a successful life and future, it is to feel free from disorganization. How can you succeed in other areas of your life if your own space at home is a mess? Have you ever noticed that when your room is messy, you can't even think right? That's because having clutter is distracting. Try putting your room in order at least once a week so you can set yourself up for success.

No. 80

Going shopping can be hard sometimes, especially when you keep trying things on but nothing looks as good on you as it does on the mannequin. Truly, who actually looks like the mannequin in the store anyway? Better to get the outfit and size that will fit you best, while flattering your own body at the same time.

No. 81

Personal hygiene plays a very important role in maintaining a healthy lifestyle. Going through puberty, adolescence and young adulthood can certainly take a toll on any girl's lifestyle. Girls get their periods at different ages and stages. So, it's crucial to recognize that showering regularly, wearing deodorant and caring for your body, including face and teeth are all important in preventing poor habits. Keeping a healthy routine is important, and it means you care about yourself!

No. 82

Becoming independent is huge in girl world! We've all been there. We might love our parents and our families, but it's also nice to have that alone time too. It's not a bad thing at all. In fact, many girls push their way out the door and pull away from their families. If you're feeling any guilt or having second thoughts about that push/pull feeling that you get inside your stomach, just know that it's perfectly normal. Parents can be annoying, friends you've been around all day at school can be annoying, and your siblings can be annoying too. Be sure that you don't push the ones you love the most too far away. It's okay to tell them that you just need some space and time for yourself. Simple as that. They'll understand because they've been there too!

No. 83

Keep a healthy lifestyle. Yes, eating healthy and working out are important. However, sometimes it can get a little old. How about making health a part of your daily routine? Don't treat it like a punishment. Do things to get your body moving every single day. For example, go on hikes, swim with friends, walk your dog. There are many fun ways to go outside and stay active without even trying!

No. 84

Procrastination. It will only get worse as you get older if you don't work on this now. When you get an assignment, schedule your time out accordingly so that you're not rushing or cramming at the last minute. Your best work will always show when you take your time on it, as opposed to just starting the night before!

No. 85

When you're at the beach or by the pool, be sure to wear sunscreen. Even though your friends may not because they want to get a little extra tan, it's important to be safe and apply it throughout the day. At the end of the day, you will be the cooler one without having that awful sunburn! Wearing sunscreen and protecting your body will keep your skin healthier as you age, and you will definitely appreciate that later on!

No. 86

Try to help your parents more often around the house with house chores. Parents do so much on a daily basis, and with work and other responsibilities, why not lend a hand and help them? Many of you might already be responsible for certain housework, and that's awesome! When everyone in the household participates as a family, it becomes appreciated, and teaches good work habits and organization – a great life skill!

No. 87

Some of you may have started driving, and some of you may be on your way! Let's just say one thing - Every teenager will learn how to drive at some point, even if he or she is not ready at the legal age. That driving test can be pretty scary. You're not alone in feeling this way. Many teenagers are skeptical at first. Driving will become second nature to you before you know it! With a lot of practice, you'll soon be prepared and have the confidence knowing the importance of being safe.

No. 88

Most young girls and young adults are overly consumed with technology and social media. Smartphones, the Internet, television, movies, music, video games. The list goes on. Every girl, no matter what age, needs a balanced lifestyle. Too much of anything can not only be habit-forming and hazardous to your health, but also affect your mood and the way your body responds to the overdosing on technology. If you seriously take a minute to think about how often you do any social media, think about all the free time you're missing out on doing a healthy, fun, physical activity to get your mind and body off the addicting computer screens!

No. 89

You know the saying … "We can choose our friends, but we can't choose our family."

Know that not every family is the perfect family. Every family has its challenges. Siblings fight, parents may argue, and it's normal. The important thing to know is that you have an important place in your family. Be grateful for the family that you have.

No. 90

How much do you think about boys? Is it daily, weekly or every second of every day? Sure, it's perfectly normal to think about the opposite gender. But, if you're consuming every waking moment of each day thinking about boys, or daydreaming in class about your crush, then most likely your distractions are the cause of you not being able to focus very well. You have plenty of time and many years for the boy thing. Right now, focus on school, friends you care about, and your family who will always be there for you. The boys will still be there and can wait.

No. 91

Do you find yourself comparing yourself to other friends' lifestyles? Do you hear about friends taking more family vacations than you? Do your friends go shopping for clothes more often than you do? Do you think friends have a better family life than you do? Their lives may appear more fabulous and exciting, but truly, no one has a perfect life. The point is, you never really know what other people are going through unless you've walked in their shoes.

No. 92

What does "charity" mean to you? How does giving back change the way you live your life? Perhaps you have a charity that you and your family donate to on a regular or yearly basis. Or, maybe it means that several times a year you donate food to a local food bank, or donate clothes to a homeless shelter. Whatever it is, the pure act of giving means you're taking positive steps in learning how to spread kindness and how to give without expecting anything in return!

No. 93

Reading is good for the soul. It doesn't matter what kind of reading materials they are. Finding books or magazines to read that spark your interest in something creates a whole new world. There are so many daily distractions, between school and extracurricular activities, events or other commitments. For anyone who says they don't like to read, they just haven't found their hidden pleasure yet! Take your mind off all the outside noise, grab a cup of hot chocolate or tea, and delve into a good read!

No. 94

If you have a sense of humor, use it! No need to keep your great personality hidden. One of the many great qualities that makes someone fun to be around is being able to make others laugh. Allow yourself to get more comfortable socially. Having a good sense of humor can sometimes help in stressful situations also. Sometimes, a great escape from the humdrum of life is being able to just laugh with your friends and take a break from all the daily stressors. Of course, every situation is different, but laughter can often be the best medicine!

No. 95

Say you're in P.E. class and you must form teams for a certain game or sport. There are usually team captains or squad leaders who will pick each person they want on their team. Don't be anxious or upset if they choose you last or close to last. You may be reading into things unnecessarily. Many times, team captains have strategically thought things through. More often than not, sometimes we let our emotions get in the way of what is really happening, and then it winds up being the opposite of what we thought. Try being more easygoing without overthinking, and just enjoy the game!

No. 96

Remember the motto, "It's Cool To Be Kind." Express random acts of kindness and show how being kind, even in the simplest of ways, can change or make someone's day. It can be as simple as giving a friend a hug, baking cookies for a neighbor, or helping a friend clean her room! Whatever it is, big or little, spread kindness and show that giving is the cool thing to do!

No. 97

Do you ever catch yourself continuously apologizing when you're speaking with other people? "Oops, I'm so sorry." "Oh my, so sorry," "Oops, my bad." Everyone makes mistakes in life, or says the wrong thing at the wrong time. Sometimes, without thinking, we can blurt things out without realizing what we said. It's important to recognize that continually apologizing in the midst of sentences makes you appear senseless. Of course, taking ownership and accountability when we say or do something wrong is a good trait, but to continually apologize is overdoing it. A good rule of thumb – think before speaking.

No. 98

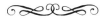

Did you know that listening to music can help clear the mind and body? It can be both relaxing and powerful at the same time. Not only does music have the ability to calm and heal, but lyrics can help build confidence. Thousands of songs sung by popular artists have inspired people all around the world. Research suggests that listening to music can help people feel better about themselves, and has many health benefits. So, start turning up the volume to your favorite tunes!

No. 99

Do you have a favorite activity you like to do? Research shows that doing an activity that you enjoy can help both your mind and body. Whether it's taking a walk with your dog, drawing or doing an art project, riding your bike, dancing in your room, or just doing something that gets you moving, it's a great mental health booster! Any activity you enjoy can also help with decreasing stress or anxiety. Take the time in engaging in something fun and exciting, either by yourself or with a friend, and you'll see how much better you'll feel!

No. 100

No need to stress over not knowing what birthday gift to buy for a friend. Sometimes creating or making a homemade gift for that special person in your life can mean so much more than purchasing any gift. Anyone can buy a gift card, but the value of a gift made especially by you will make it that more special. There are tons of gift creation ideas online. So, start looking up all the unique DIY gift items on Pinterest or YouTube videos. It might just spark some creative juices and talent you never thought you had in you!

No. 101

Have you ever surprised a family member or friend just for the sake of making them feel good or special? Not because it's their birthday or anniversary, but just because. Gift giving on a whim is sometimes the best gift of all! It could be picking flowers from your own garden and giving it to that special person in your life, or writing someone a thank you note for being such a good friend. As corny as it might appear, your small, kind gesture just might make someone's entire day!

My Journey Follows

Made in the USA
San Bernardino, CA
14 June 2017